SPRINGSTEEN
LIVE

SPRING

Photographs by Philip Kamin

Text by Peter Goddard

STEEN LIVE

NEW ENGLISH LIBRARY

BRITISH LIBRARY CATALOGUING IN
PUBLICATION DATA

Kamin, Philip
Springsteen: live

1. Springsteen, Bruce   2. Rock musicians—
—United States—Biography
I. Title   II. Goddard, Peter
784.5′ 0092   ML420.S77

ISBN 0-450-05752-6

First published in Canada by Stoddart
Publishing, a Division of General Publishing
Co. Limited, Toronto.

First NEL Paperback Edition
February 1985

NEL Books are published by
New English Library
Mill Road, Dunton Green,
Sevenoaks, Kent.
Editorial Office:
47 Bedford Square
London WC1B 3DP

ISBN 0 450 05752 6

Design/Newton Frank
Printed in Canada

ACKNOWLEDGEMENTS

Special thanks to Allan Stokell at Positive Images; Tom at MCPL for the excellent development of the black & white prints; Leo Robichaud, Doug Paddey, Marty Ingles & Gary Beck at Canon Cameras of Canada; Bob, Glen, Skip, Nancy, Erica & Margo at Steichenlab, Toronto, for the quality development of the color transparencies.

P.K.

———————————————————

To Ron Base, Bruce Blackadar and their midnights with The Boss.

For Philip . . . and of course C.A. and Kate.

P.G.

"The main secret about singing ain't so much to have other folks listen to you as it is to pick up your own spirits."
— Woody Guthrie

So there's Bruce Springsteen and he's dancing, folks. He's video so this live footage was needed to take advantage of a hit song, *Dancing In The Dark*, hit album, *Born In The U.S.A.* and hit worldwide tour. The girl dances once more and De Palma catches it.

through the dark curtains backstage and up on to the stage itself. This difference is slight but it is noticeable. He's been exercising back home in New Jersey, running every day and lifting weights. The old white T-shirt he wears, sleeves rolled tight and high over his biceps, is now stretched where it used to merely hang. "Now he really *does* look like a mechanic from New Jersey," says a critic who flew in for the shows from Dallas.

Nor does he use the stage as one vast runway for what used to be his perpetual flight during his mammoth three-hour shows. The shows are just as long and they're just as richly textured but what he does with them—and during them—is quite different.

They're a lot more focused on the center of the stage—not on him running about, but just on him. They're more personal. He opens up more. He's laughing more. You feel closer. Night after night you'll hear him talking about . . . well, himself: about Freehold, N.J., and growing up; about his dad and driving around his hometown and playing baseball as a kid. You learn more about Bruce Springsteen this time out than you had learned all the times he'd

ures but it wasn't a night with all of the old and so very terribly *serious* passion. The "future of rock'n'roll" is now very much its standard. Springsteen's made his point. These nights he's a lot less frantic than he'd been in past tours, but maybe he's accomplishing a lot more. These nights the songs sell the singer, not the singer his songs.

Yet there's something glorious in all this. There always is with him. Something very American. Imagine a parade that stays in one spot with all its flags flying, or an entire political convention dedicated to one and only one man. Imagine a small-town high school pageant done Hollywood style. Now try to imagine all these things together and you'll get an idea of what the *Born In The U.S.A.* tour is about. It's rock'n'roll and a lot more as well. It's something as grand and glorious as an act of faith.

Springsteen wants a role to play as much as he wants a crowd to play to. He's paid attention to Woody Guthrie's life. At the beginning of his career he was aiming to be the soul for rock'n'roll—"When I was nine and saw Elvis Presley on TV, I knew that was where it was at," he once said. But that has

I mean, I *like* it but I don't know if I should approve of it. Two-thirds of the crowd around me some nights watched most of the show on the screen and yet Bruce Springsteen is the consummate live performer.)

But it's still true that the most effective pieces are the ones where the technology doesn't matter and where the cheering has to stop. *My Hometown* is hardly a song for partying. It is as much about urban decay as it is the decay of dreams. It is played with a fleet, effortless grace—you want to let it flow past you, that's all—but its theme simply cannot be ignored. And there's often a great and sudden quiet for some of the other darker songs, like *Johnny 99* or *Atlantic City* from *Nebraska*. Look out into the crowd, especially at those determined to have a good time, and you can see the lyrics' intent reflected in their faces. They're listening. It's as if everyone has come to a luxurious dinner party only to be lectured by the host on the plight of starving nations.

As the hot young stud singer out of Asbury, N.J., Springsteen started out as the '70s answer to Bob Dylan. He's gone on to become the 1980s answer to . . . well, only one thing

bopping and jiving to his own tune, *Dancing In The Dark*, and he's looking our way, over to the side of the stage. And such a grin. Bruce Springsteen has a jaw no boxer should have. It's a strong jaw but it sticks out, the perfect target for a jab. And when he grins this jaw looks like it has put his face into a clamp. Anyhow, he has a woman up there with him and they're dancing some sort of basement boogie when I happen to notice this balding guy with a beard watching them.

Intently. I can almost *hear* this fellow sweat. He's right at the edge of the stage, heavy-set, yet he moves quickly, getting the angle, nudging the cameraman closer and closer to the singer. There's something angry in the way his body moves; it's as if this guy would be just as willing to go through a wall as around it.

A PR guy nudges closer and says, "That's Brian De Palma." The director of *Carrie* and *Dressed To Kill* is shooting Springsteen's new video, and just in case the first run-through of the piece doesn't work they are doing it again. Springsteen's management did in fact reject the idea of a concert

But then it's done and that great whoosh of crowd roar washes over the stage and the director and crew huddled at the side of the stage. They can barely hear each other talk but a guard at the side of the stage asks De Palma, "Did you get it?"

"Yeah," says the director. "Yeah."

So once again Bruce Springsteen heads out into an America he imagines in his songs, and once again everyone's out there waiting for him. Right now we're in St. Paul, and here are nearly 40,000 tickets have gone for the tour's very first three shows at the Civic Center. It's much the same *every-where*. His plans include gigs in the New York City area alone for a month. There aren't many places on this planet he's *not* playing through 1984 and 1985.

But something *is* different this time out, nonetheless. This is not the same country he discovered when last out on the road (especially not here in "quality-of-life" country where a crowd full of smiling blond young people turned out for his shows—now it is where Prince lives and where his movie "Purple Rain" was shot).

But then again, Springsteen's not the same singer either. Or the same person.

He's heavier for one thing. More muscular. You notice this as he leads his band out

toured before. And you learn it from him, not from a bevy of writers. This time out he'll be the one to interpret himself.

A little later on during the tour the huge video screen above the stage was used to greater effect, and it became more and more evident just how intimate Springsteen and audience had become in this most panoramic of rock shows. But it was no less physical a show. This will *always* be a show about sweat and tears, and muscles and heat.

But the nature of its physicality had changed. One night in particular it was well past halfway into the concert when the crowd gave Bruce what was going to be the biggest cheer in this long, muggy, ecstatic night.

It came with *Dancing In The Dark*, but it wasn't because the song is a hit on pop radio. Nor was it because he ended up dancing with a young women in the audience who simply wouldn't stop hugging him. ("It's the toughest part of this job," he kidded.)

No, it was because there, on the huge video screen suspended from a crane over the stage . . . there, bigger than all outdoors, in glowing color too, was a shot of his . . . bottom.

Well, yes indeed! How perfect. How typical. For this was a night of long-lasting generosity and many pleas-

led him to something more demanding and complicated. Nine years have passed and four albums have been recorded since he released *Born To Run*, and Springsteen has become the newest version of the oldest kind of working-class hero—a hustler of the every-day-dream. And it's something everyone knows, something everyone last night went along with.

There's a bit of the small-town booster club to these concerts. There's a bit of the pep rally to them, too. Everyone sings *Hungry Heart* as the band plays on. This song is communal property now—far more communal than most folk songs. And as everyone sings it, it's as if he's up there onstage just to cheer us along. Everywhere I look I can see people smiling. As we bounce in our seats to the rocker, *Cadillac Ranch*, no one feels blitzed-out, wacko or crazy. Everyone's happy—it's just as simple as that.

As odd as it might sound, though—I mean, what's wrong with happiness?—there may be some consternation in all of this. There's a gap growing between what his music is all about and what his concerts are all about. It seems that the happier and more technologically assured his concerts become, the darker his music grows.

(I'm still not sure that I like this huge video screen—

actually: what he himself was doing in the '70s. His band these nights—led by a slimmer Clarence Clemons, and comprised of so many of the same musicians he's always had—nevertheless sounds more freeway stream-lined than an E Street shuffle.

Once this band concocted a great happy jumble of sound but now it's richer and sleeker. *Dancing In The Dark* passes across the stage like some vast stretch limo. It glides out on a synthesizer line as rich as a French horn solo as Bruce croons the words. But listen, the modern touches don't stop there. At one point, the same video camera catches his feet in mid-dance step—the influence of Michael Jackson, perhaps?

In some ways, this tour continues on from where the last one left off, just as in some ways *Born In The U.S.A.* and *Nebraska* carry on from where *The River* left off. I used to think of him as one of rock's last innocents—you know, the kid dreaming about the ultimate road machine, the ultimate girl to go along with it, the endless highway and the endless night—who came out of nowhere in the seventies—well, Asbury Park, New Jersey—to bring an old kind of righteousness back to American music. But his shows this time out are too big and have too much hinging on them for that.

U.S.A.'s release much earlier. They had to bide their time while the singer and the producers—Jon Landau (his manager), Chuck Plotkin and Miami Steve Van Zandt—kept retooling the production. But if there were troubles leading up to the album's release, there's nothing troubled about the music itself. To be frightfully simplistic about it, this is the album where Bruce Springsteen gets the car but loses the girl. Sex has come to rival escape as the theme—sex and, of course, work. Springsteen and his friend Bob Seger are two of the very few singers who regard work as material for music.

The sensual side of things is emphasized even before you get to the music. The cover photo is a shot of the singer's behind. He's wearing old, torn blue jeans. A red hat sticks out of one pocket. His photo on the inside sleeve is possibly the most directly sexy ever taken as he stands, chest out, legs apart, in a white T-shirt and jeans (leave Pepsi to Michael Jackson: Springsteen should get Levi's to sponsor him). As for the music? A few pieces come directly from the established Springsteen mold: *Born In The U.S.A.*, *Bobby Jean* and *No Surrender*. *Dancing In The Dark*, the current single and the subject of his first video ever, is also typical Springsteen (the

called *Bobby Jean*. It's about a friendship, a shattered friendship between a man and a woman, and for reasons I can't pretend to understand it got beneath my skin in a way no other piece on this album has done.

Born In The U.S.A. arrived with much ballyhoo in a season of ballyhoo. It was a season of blockbusters, from the Los Angeles Olympics to "Indiana Jones and the Temple of Doom" to the

The National Education Association was in town, about 10,500 educators strong, but they had to be in conference or class or whatever this afternoon, because the bar was nearly empty. I probably would have been playing the Little Casino Poker game over there in the corner, or watching the bartender shift bottles around, Seagram's to the right, Beefeater next on the left, or listening to the

His new songs—from the two-year-old *Nebraska* and *Born in the U.S.A.* albums—are more Born to Worry than Born to Run.

But let's back up for a moment to the Twin Cities, where it's all starting. This deep vein of concern running through his songs is overlooked one in from the suburbs—Lake Harriet, Burl Oaks or Kenwood—thinks this is great, and nothing but great. They're up and on their feet waving tanned arms in the air. St. Paul, along with (twin city) Minneapolis, is so nice and wholesome that, as the joke around here goes, it's the kind of company your mother always wanted you to keep. This, I don't think, is exactly the working-class America Springsteen is singing about. What it is is the America that scores high in "quality-of-life polls."

The starkness of his songs cannot be ignored. These songs, as *Newsweek* critic Bill Barol noted awhile ago, "picture an America gone deeply wrong." Yet, in much the same way, the rapture at his concerts can't be dismissed either. If his live shows reflect anything, it's not anything gone wrong, but a night going extremely right. You can argue that his shows themselves aren't about the America he is singing about; that there's that gap between what he does and how he does it;

Shuffle. The fans are here, as one woman I met before the show had told me, "not to go crazy but to listen." But lately too there are folks who have just been discovering him, and in truth a kind of sweet craziness is what *this* part of the crowd is after.

So he works both audiences with both kinds of songs. For example, two spotlights crisscross on his face as he sings *I'm On Fire*. It's a new song about an old subject—midnight passion—and it's done in what is for him a new intimate way; more of a lusty murmur than anything else. It is remarkably personal and it seems to have been stylized for his older audience. It leads directly to an older song, *Fire*, and an older mood. And it all became one glorious sing-along. Whenever he would be about to sing the song's title, he would back away from the microphone to let the crowd bellow out, "Fii-re."

During some of the final shows of *The River* tour, his last time out in 1981, he'd mentioned he had been reading about America and in particular Joe Klein's *Woody Guthrie—A Life*. His concern for America has obviously deepened. At one point late into the show here he talked "freedom."

But there is another kind of concern at work here too—concern about him. One Twin Cities' critic, Rick Shefchik, wondered in a

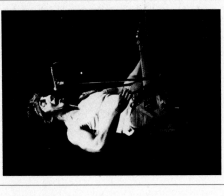

that the songs are about isolation—but only on occasion during live performances is this starkness captured.

But the moment you see the E Street Band spread across the stage, you see a panoramic version of the rock and roll club act. There's Nils Lofgren, the guitarist brought in to replace long-time friend Miami Steve Van Zandt, now out with his own band. Lofgren is gradually fitting in closer and closer with the core of a band that's been with Springsteen for nearly a decade. There's Clarence Clemons, looking simultaneously thinner, younger, happier. And there's the core of the band: Danny Federici and Roy Bittan, the keyboard players; drummer Max Weinberg; and bassist Garry Tallent. As well, there's Patti Scialfa, who might be described as a very upfront back-up singer. (When I see her backstage a little later, I almost don't recognize her. It has nothing to do with her appearance but with attitude—she seems as buoyed up by the show as the crowd.)

Right now, though, standing backstage as the band pours out the exuberant *Glory Days*, I can see the same faces Springsteen sees. And they're ecstatic from beginning to end. Part of this audience has grown up with him, right from 1973 and the days of *The Wild, The Innocent And The E Street*

piece he'd written, "Who is Bruce Springsteen now? [He'd] like to crawl into our skins and bear some of the same pain, but in doing so he crawls out of his own and loses his identity completely."

But another critic, D. L. Mabery, came up with a possible answer. It is found in his songs. "Where his epic heroes were once teenage kids in search of grandeur," wrote Mabery, "here they are characters caught in the process of becoming adults."

Thompson Twins endlessly playing on the box, but instead I was getting terribly melancholy talking to Paula.

Now, Paula figures in here because she wears Bruce Springsteen on her sleeve, right where her heart should be. She'd seen me reading about him, so we started talking only to discover that we'd seen the very same Springsteen show in Chicago in 1980—a concert where he'd read to the crowd a letter he'd received asking him to play at a local wedding. So we talked about that too.

But something was unsettling Paula. Every twenty minutes or so she'd head out into the lobby to make a phone call—a tall, big-boned woman, in clean faded blue jeans and a man's working shirt. She was phoning her sister to see how her son was. He'd just come down with something—"he's a little feverish" she said—and she was worried. Actually, she felt guilty. She felt guilty, she said, because here she was going to a Bruce Springsteen concert while her ill child was at home.

I ordered two more glasses of white wine as she headed back out to the phone. Because of her sadness, and because Springsteen was in the air, I started thinking about a tune on the new album, as sweet a bit of melancholy as you can find

I was reading all this about Springsteen the afternoon of the opening show of the tour while sitting at the bar in the Radisson St. Paul Hotel. But in truth, there wasn't all that much to read so I started to watch the bartender slice melons. (It's the kind of bar where exotic drinks of Polynesian inclination are available, so lots of fruit has to be on hand.)

As to why there wasn't that much to read—well, the Twin Cities area took Springsteen's arrival quite casually. Some kids hung around the silver semi's parked outside the Civic Center, girls mostly, looking more bored than anxious. But that was about it. The star wasn't talking so all that was left to writers and critics was speculation and criticism, all of it stemming from the *Born In The U.S.A.* album.

Jacksons' Victory Tour. Everything was bigger than big. There was the new Jacksons' album, *Victory*, and Prince's *Purple Rain*, but Springsteen's twelve-song collection, wrapped in the stars and bars of the American flag, was definitely one of pop's heavy-hitters.

That is, from the sales point of view. As music it is many things, but not heavy in any sense of the word. It's probably his most deft, skillful and incisive work yet. Anyhow, CBS Records shipped out large quantities in advance and radio stations were playing cuts from *Born In The U.S.A.* night and day.

Its arrival could not have been better timed, coming just as his tour got underway. Nonetheless, the album had its share of troubles getting here. *Nebraska*, the stark, acoustic work which preceded it, didn't sell well. Worse, it wasn't played on rock radio. Springsteen's obsession with the hard times of blue-collar America wasn't appreciated (even if it *was* understood) by an industry prepped up by Reagan optimism. Its poor sales left music industry insiders wondering if Springsteen had lost his touch—that is, if he'd lost sight of what he'd set out to do. He hadn't, as it turned out.

But then to complicate matters, CBS executives had expected *Born In The*

full band sound, thick textures, a beat halfway between a dance and a march) except it has been streamlined somewhat. Then there are those themes he still mulls over. He's still sitting outside one house or another in his car. Waiting and thinking. Despite all his talk about hitting the road, Springsteen's real passion is waiting and thinking.

He's waiting and thinking outside Bobby Jean's house and again in the very next song, *I'm Goin' Down*, except here he's waiting *with* the girl, not *for* her. Women are still a problem, though. If the girl doesn't leave him, he takes her away only to find her brothers, father or the sheriff showing up to take her back again.

So much for what you might call the expected. It's in the unexpected where the wonders lie. *Working On The Highway* is a superbly crafted bit of modern rock-

meant—"he's about the only male singer I know who doesn't seem to dislike women. I mean, women can listen to his songs and not have to deal with the masculine viewpoint? You understand what I mean?"

I said I did. "But something was wrong with Phil and I," she went on. The bar was beginning to fill up with educators and we had to talk quietly. "I remember getting all excited when *The River* came out and we sat around listening to it one night and he ended up crying. He was always unhappy. I don't know how I got pregnant then but I did. I think that made it worse. I tried to get him to talk about it but he couldn't. Or wouldn't. I don't know. I asked him if there was another woman, but there wasn't he said. I thought maybe he was gay or something but he said that I was being stupid.

"You know what it was? I think he was just worried—worried about me, about the baby, about everything. He was worried about everything. Things had caught up to him and he felt trapped, I guess.

"He didn't leave me. He just drifted away. He got a house nearby then he moved into an apartment here in St. Paul and then he moved to another apartment. He used to visit Joey—that's our son—on the weekends. He was always a good father.

abilly. *Downbound Train* is simply haunting—he sings an entire verse backed only by horn-like synthesizers. Finally, there's *I'm On Fire* which hints at rockabilly but has the finely drawn shape of a classic folk song. In fact, many of these songs have the kind of elegant simplicity which indicates not just a good song writer but an exceptional one.

As for rockers, there are some bits here and there—the start of *Goin' Down* or most of *Darlington County*—which have the dramatic passion (and a bit of the Rolling Stones sound) of the Rolling Stones at their best. But so what. This is Springsteen at *his* best I think—and for reasons that have little to do with all the shopworn notions about his songs. I like pop. I accept its limitations because its the struggle against these limitations which produces much of its dynamism. Springsteen has never set such restrictions upon himself as he's done in *Born In The U.S.A.* There's no sprawl in his songs. Everything's lean—even all the sentiment. And yet he's never gone so far with his writing. I don't think he's ever stretched out quite as much.

Never have his abilities as a craftsman been so evident before. And never has his craft been at the service of so much feeling. There's an erotic pulse behind that dull throb of pain in *Bobby Jean* but he's managed to keep it at a distance where it doesn't get in the way of what he's saying but where it also won't be forgotten. Women may hear the song differently than men, but most men I know who've heard it have had a *Bobby Jean* in their lives: she was their buddy and sometimes they went to shows together or studied together or went on long walks together and sometimes they slept together but in the end that didn't matter as much as their friendship.

Paula came back to say her kid was okay—at least her sister *said* he was okay—and so she wasn't going to worry any more. She didn't expect me to believe her of course, so I didn't.

I remember an uncle of mine telling me something about how he got through World War II: about how he cannot remember actually marching around northern France although he was there for two years, and he can't remember the fighting. What he can remember is "the soft times, the easy times"—the girls he'd met and the music he'd heard on the hit parade back then. "It was if we were fighting *inside* those songs, you understand?" he said one day. "I can still hear every note of *String Of Pearls* played by the Glenn Miller band. For me, back then, it was everything, everything— the dance back home I wanted to be at, the girl I wanted at that dance, the car we'd drive home in, the porch, the front door, the light over the door. That song was home."

In much the same way, another generation has grown up living inside Springsteen's songs. Some people anyway, and Paula, as it turned out, was one of them.

"It wasn't me so much at first but my husband—my *ex*-husband," she said. "He was the one who heard Bruce first, when he was into his acoustic thing. I didn't particularly like him then—Bruce, I mean. I've always like my ex-husband.

"I'm from Boston originally and I met Phil when he was at school there. He was going to be a statistician and he hated it. I was a teacher and I felt trapped. So we decided to head to New Hampshire, you know, to get back to the earth."

She smiled at that. She was ready-made to be called an earth mother—tall, slightly plump, with great strong hands. She drank some wine. "Well, we both found we didn't *like* getting back to the earth. But we also knew we didn't want to live in the city so we moved out here. Phil found some work he liked—there's lots of new industry around here. And we decided to fix up an old farmhouse we'd found. Jesus, did we work hard at that house. I taught part-time and we'd both get back to pull down walls or nail up boards. It was always a mess. Always. I don't think we were ever happier.

"And we'd listen to Springsteen—*Born To Run*. We'd rip nails and sing along to *Thunder Road*. We'd hammer and saw and sing some more to *Jungleland* and drink some wine and we'd get totally exhausted and fall into bed and make love. God it was wonderful that year. I remember we went to Chicago once—it was a holiday weekend—and we were walking along Michigan Avenue. People kept stopping to look at us. Actually, they were looking at Phil. He was really tanned and really handsome and I hoped he'd never find out how good lookin' he was. He looked just like a movie star. Like Tom Selleck.

"We finally got the house fixed up and by then I was really into Springsteen. I thought I was too old to feel as attached to any singer as I was to him but I couldn't wait until his next album was out. I loved everything about *Darkness On The Edge Of Town*—*Candy's Room* particularly. It reminded me of me."

It was about 5 p.m. now, and the concert wasn't too long away. We'd ordered some more wine. "You want to know something about him?" —Springsteen, she meant. "But he stopped visiting after a while. I've been really worried about him for some time. I bought *Nebraska* and I felt I was listening inside Phil's head. I felt I was living inside a Bruce Springsteen song. I've never known music that could get to me this way.

"The funny thing is, though, things were getting better. It was Phil who got the tickets to this show tonight. He phoned up out of the blue and asked me if I'd like to go with him."

I put some money out on the counter but she pushed it aside. "But I guess not," she went on. "I feel I've gone on. I don't think he has, that's all. Springsteen is still important for me. I think he's saying something important in his new album. But Phil—well, he phoned again to say he wouldn't be making it. So I was stuck with the tickets. I was going to invite a friend but it was too late. Besides, I want to keep it as a souvenir."

She had to pick up a few things before stores closed she told me, so I said I'd walk her to her car just down the street. We said goodbye outside the Amherst H. Wilder Foundation Senior Citizen's Center. The weather was sticky.

"It's something we all have to go through," said Paula, squinting in the light outside the bar. "I'm just glad I've got this ticket."

at CBS will tell you.

The real reason, however, was that the singer started hassling with his ex-manager Mike Appel and the resulting legal wrangle brought his career to an abrupt halt. When Appel's attorney, Leonard Marks, announced finally that the ten-month squabble was over, both the manager and the singer emerged with what they wanted—Appel with a cash settlement and a five-year production deal from Columbia, and Springsteen with control of his own music publishing, unused tapes, a 1975 concert film made in England, and a new album, *Darkness On The Edge Of Town*. Springsteen, in short, was his own man.

"It was a silly thing," he says about his legal difficulties. "I was told I could do anything I wanted to do—but only to a certain point. Well, I had to get out of that kind of arrangement."

He's sitting upright on the edge of a couch in a cold, concrete room somewhere in the bowels of the gymnasium. It's a truly ugly room and he's ignoring it totally. When he talks, his eyes narrow. He has his harmonica in his right hand and, from time to time, he brandishes it as if to punctuate his sentences.

"I always had trouble with business, though. Part of the reason I went into rock'n'roll was to avoid business. If I'd wanted to be a businessman I'd have been a shoe salesman. To this day I'm still bad at it. But, hey! I can't help it. Worrying about business takes all the fun out of it. All I want to do is play a show, run around onstage, and go on to the next show.

"Not that I wasn't playing during all those . . . hassles. I'd save a bit of money, but just a bit, plus I had the big expense of keeping the group together. So every so often we'd head out on the road, to the South or Midwest, and do three or four shows just to keep some money coming in. At one point, though, they tried to attach the box-office receipts. But we got by."

The time away did more than straighten out his business affairs. It took the pressure off—the pressure from the media, from his record company and, most of all, from his fans, who looked to his music for answers they couldn't find elsewhere.

"I was always scared stiff by those kinds of questions," he says. "I never had the answer to anybody's life. I don't have the answer to my

Durham, New Hampshire, Late Fall, 1978

He has just finished three hours onstage, almost nonstop, jumping on amps, jumping on boxes, sliding along the stage, landing cold and hard on his knees after some wrenching leaps. Sweat spewed from his face, arms and neck, soaking everything near him. And he has just wiped out a crowd of kids who packed into the Lundholm Gymnasium at the University of New Hampshire.

Wiped them out! They're only now heading back into the darkness at the center of town, back to the Kappa Epsilon house for a few final beers, back to the dorms to wring out their "The Boss Is Back" T-shirts. Wiped 'em! They're just drifting shadows on the road now, but here and there you can hear them singing his choice lines about hey, baby, being "born to run."

"But it's just starting for me — the night," says Bruce Springsteen as he walks along a corridor in the gym's basement. He moves gingerly, as if his feet hurt — as well they might, this being the 65th stop in a 125-concert tour.

"Nights like these don't tire me. Nights like these make me go. The kids at places like these go nuts. They think it's Santa Claus. "You get anxious before the show, just because of the people and what they're expecting. It's their night. But that anxiousness, that tension, is good. It's good for rock'n'roll. Each show has such intensity it's as if it's the end of the world. But it's the only way I have to validate what I do."

Classic Springsteen, this. But it still feels unexpected from the lithe singer with the olive-colored skin, the single, tiny pearl earring, and the look of a hungry New York actor playing the part of his career. Just three years ago, he had it all. Rock critic Jon Landau, who later went on to produce his third album, Born To Run, wrote enthusiastically that he "saw the rock and roll future and its name is Bruce Springsteen." And Michael Watts, an English critic, said that he listened to Springsteen "like I used to listen to Dylan, John Lennon and Chuck Berry — like my life depended on it."

Springsteen had become "It" — the '70s answer to the Beatles, the great new thing in rock'n'roll, the embodiment of all its blood and thunder and street-primed funk. He was the answer. He looked like any one of the dudes who hung out in pool halls in his hometown of Freehold, N.J. He loved power in his cars and vintage rock. The music of Phil Spector, The Ronettes and early, very early, Dylan was in his blood.

Dig it! In the same week in October, 1975, both Newsweek and Time did full-bore Springsteen cover stories, both probing and contributing to the hype that was welling up around him.

"Both pieces were written by people who had been fans for a long time," said Bruce Lundvall, a CBS Records vice-president in New York, trying to explain the media overkill.

But why not? With lines like "I could walk like Brando," or "I had skin like leather and the diamond-hard look of a cobra," Springsteen was great copy. He was the romance of rock come alive. In his music everyone heard echoes of American street-heroes, from James Dean to Buddy Holly to Joey in "On The Waterfront." Better yet, he seemed to be the real thing. He was sincere. Everyone said so. He was the faith of rock and roll.

Of course, all of this just pumped hot air into a balloon that was bound to burst. And it did, not long after all the publicity appeared. He didn't tour, didn't record. He disappeared. It wasn't because his fans or the press were suddenly turned off. Although his first two albums, Greetings From Asbury Park and The E Street Shuffle, sold poorly, the much-publicized Born To Run release "just took off," people I'd driven up from Boston in a rented car and had no idea about who or what I'd meet. I'd seen him onstage before but always through a screen of absolutely nutsy fans who didn't seem to be actually listening to the music as participating in it. And, in truth, I had my suspicions. I felt my feeling about him and his music had been manipulated. Foremost, he was someone to discover — that impelling, thick voice of his hurling images in my ears.

"The reason I started playing guitar when I was fourteen was to be my own man. That's the reason I got into music," he says. "So why should I have someone telling me what I could do? The music came before the money, so it was important to get as much control as possible so you could make the music.

"I guess what happened to me is just something that slips up on all of us. When you're playing and aren't making any money, these problems don't come up. But, when you become a valuable property," — he says "property" — as if it's a joke and laughs as he says it — "people want as much as they can possibly get from you. The record company wants as many records as possible. People want money. And you start to feel everything slipping out from underneath — you lose control.

own. But I don't think the kids are interested in that kind of thing any more. That was what happened in the '60s; '60s people thought there were answers — later, people realized there aren't any.

"You're just here to perform. There are no answers beyond that. You're just thumbing your way through the dark looking for that light spot."

Go to enough of his concerts over the years and you'll hear all you'll ever need to know about Bruce Springsteen. Night after night the story is developed, now in a song, now in a bit of rap between songs — opera almost, aria and recitative, drama and development. It's very Italian, this. Like Verdi or something. He says he gets his love for storytelling from his mother, Adele's side of the family, the Zirillis, the Italian side of his family. (His father's (Douglas's) side is Dutch — the colony was first brought under English rule in 1664, but the Dutch disputed the claim for the next five years.)

But there's another factor here as well. He reads history. And he certainly knows the shape and scope of a history well told. Among his most complete songs, those pieces with absolutely no loose ends to them, are

worry much about money, as he remarked in his autobiography (written with Irving Townsend), *John Hammond On The Record*. In fact, on meeting him you're given the impression that he doesn't worry much about anything—except, perhaps, music. The bosses at CBS, I remember him telling me, "Put up with me because I'm always coming up with people when they least expect it."

As nervous as he was for the audition, Springsteen so impressed Hammond that he was signed with CBS within a day. There was, of course a small problem here, though. CBS saw him as an acoustic act and Springsteen needed to convince them that he'd spent most of his adult life in a band. *Greetings From Asbury Park*, the first album, reflects somewhat this double-vision. It can be heard as an acoustic album with a band, or a band album with acoustic music threaded through it. No matter, it was the end of the beginning for him.

"Don't ask why," he continues on in this chilly basement. "My life started when I was fourteen and got my first guitar. I see my life in two parts. Before I was fourteen I did nothing. After it I did one thing—played the guitar and performed. I never was a big reader, and although I like movies a lot I don't have much time for

authority than the *Encyclopedia Britannic* describes its "urban garishness." It is, of course, perfect rock'n'roll territory.

But before he could get there, semi-permanently at least, little Bruce Springsteen had to endure school, growing up and coming to terms with his father and still more growing up. Early on he felt like a misfit at school. He went to a Catholic school where the nuns wouldn't accept his misfit, rock'n'roll rebel ways. He was forever being kicked out of class. He was forever being scolded, at home and school. It did little good—except, maybe, yielding a number of songs for him. Right from the start he knew that if he was going to make it, it wouldn't be through school or because of school. Right from the start, he knew he wanted to be a rock'n'roller.

He'd considered sports, baseball particularly, but soon enough realized his talents took him in a different direction. (Although he picked up surfing along the way and becoming quite good at it.) So he played blues and heavy metal, Who-like power chords and soon developed a reputation as a hot guitarist. The Upstage Club was the place in Asbury Park but he was playing in New York clubs as well. Along the way he met more and more of the musicians

those which could be called histories.

Sometimes, you'll learn a lot from what he leaves out — the parts which sometimes end up in his songs.

Freehold N.J., where he grew up—first-born in a family that would have as well two girls, Ginny and Pam—was and still is to some degree a town in con-

stant flux. In this regard, the Springsteen family was somewhat typical. His father changed jobs often and houses almost as often although this was in no way particular in a state where people were always on the move looking for something better, chasing jobs, homes, looking for the way up or out. Younger couples moved to the suburbs from the cities: old industry being abandoned for new.

Restless always, Douglas Springsteen would go out for long drives. Driving would be among his son's favorite recreations as well. In this and at least one other way father and son are very much alike: both are loners, needing to be by themselves at times. The father moved to California in 1969, eventually driving bus in Sean Mateo. The son stayed behind.

One of the few constants in all of this has been the Jersey shore, a 127-mile strip along the Atlantic which begins in the south with Cape May, reputedly the oldest resort in the Americas. The shore has always been used for one sort of escape or another and Asbury Park was in the business of cheap thrills. It's pinball parlors and music played loud; the smell of vinegar, salt and pepper on chips. Salt air. People are not kind in their descriptions of Asbury Park. No less an

who'd end up in his bands, as well as his first manager, Tinker West. Tinker West made surfboards and encouraged Springsteen's band at the time, Steel Mill, to play California. Its west coast tour, so-called, was brief and the band ended up back in New Jersey. Bruce soon disbanded it, forming Dr. Zoom and the Sonic Boom. Tinker West meanwhile had met the song-writing team of Mike Appel and Jim Cretecos— they were moderately commercially successful, having penned the Partridge Family hit, *Doesn't Somebody Want To Be Wanted?* Springsteen played for them and Appel was knocked out with what he heard, and eventually arranged an audition for his new client with John Hammond, of CBS Records. To Springsteen, Hammond was a legend. He'd read about him in Anthony Scudato's biography of Bob Dylan and could barely imagine meeting the man who discovered Billie Holiday as well as Dylan. This was the man who'd supervised Fletcher Henderson's first recording for Columbia and produced Bessie Smith's last. He'd help put Count Basie's band together. He'd supported Benny Goodman–his brother-in law—throughout the clarinetist's career.

John Henry Hammond was born the great-great grandson of *the* Cornelius Vanderbilt. He never had to

'em. I'm just a regular stiff. I have no hobbies outside of playing or writing.

"But the way I see it, if you're going to do one thing and do it well, you can't allow a lot of distractions. When I first picked up that guitar it was—well, it was like walking through the gates. That was it for me.

"Rock'n'roll gave me everything and I feel I have everything to give in return. It's like a pact. A vow. And you have to honor it. Sometimes I work so hard onstage I can lose two or three pounds a show—and I haven't got many pounds to lose. At one point earlier this year my weight went from 153 to 139 pounds but it didn't really affect me physically, although I don't eat, hardly. I don't do drugs, don't drink— so I'm okay.

"It's hard to explain what happens when you get onstage. You're full of tension before you go on and the minute you hear that crowd your stomach tenses. It goes hard, just like those bodybuilders who pump up their muscles and it stays that way through the show. Sometimes I feel like I'm going to throw up.

"But I know this: the day I can't go on, I'm finished. I'm dead. I mean, you don't have much time in life, so why waste it. And if you have something to say, there has to be some urgency in the way you say it."

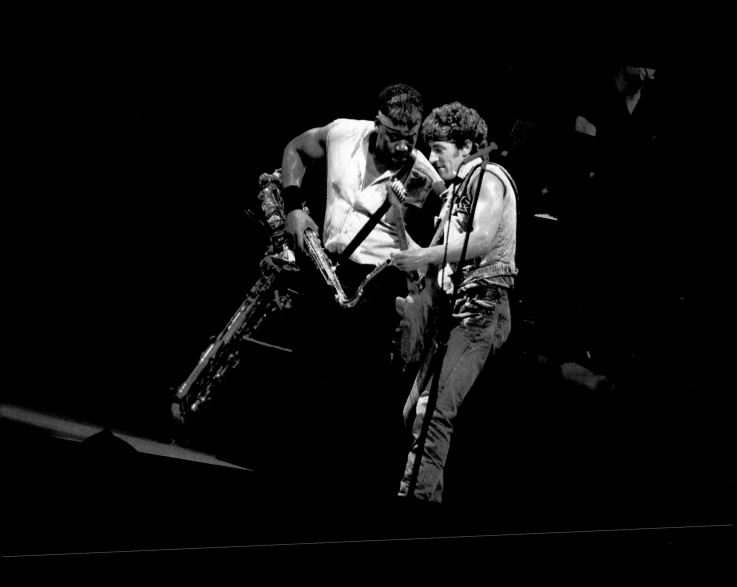

When he wasn't touring, part of his band was.

Max Weinberg, the drummer with his own book about drummers, *The Big Beat*, to his credit, was telling me one afternoon how hard the E Street Band plays—how everyone has to be totally on top of what they're doing all the time. This is, of course, the kind of band that almost needs to play this way, like a high-performance car needs a lot of top-speed road work. So as Springsteen worked through *Born In The U.S.A.*, others headed out on their own. But why not? The E Street Band had spawned its own stars, first among which, one might suppose, is the Big Man.

"When he's making changes on his album, I've had the time to do what I've always liked to do."

Clarence Clemons is talking about his sometime employer, Bruce Springsteen. What Clemons is also talking about is touring along with his own band, the Red Bank Rockers.

With Springsteen, Clemons takes on a special character onstage. Physically, they've always been each other's foil—Clarence, the solid one, moving little; Springsteen, always in flight. This has hardly changed even though Clemons has dropped weight and styled his hair and Springsteen has added some muscle. Springsteen used to tell a story about how he and Miami Steve met Clarence late one night on the boardwalk and how absolutely scary Clarence had seemed, a big guy in a white suit. Well, the new Clarence is more benevolent than scary. He beams down at the crowd sort of like everyone's older brother—the kind of older brother who lets the kid, Springsteen, fool around.

Being Springsteen's sidekick and chief sideman is a mixed blessing. It brings you more attention than you'll ever need. (No early photo of Springsteen was complete without showing him leaning up against the sax player—an image made famous by the cover of the *Born To Run* album). Clemons even ended up in a bit role in Martin Scorsese's movie, "New York, New York" (as a trumpet player!). He landed a recording contract with CBS and this, in turn, enabled him to tour last year.

On the other hand, there's the lingering suspicion—on the part of critics, if not on his own part—that he's basking in Springsteen's shadow. As if to only confuse the issue a bit more, in the video released a while back for the song *A Woman's Got The Power*, Springsteen makes an appearance. The album *Rescue* included a Springsteen song and a Springsteen co-production for the piece *Savin' Up*. The Boss is even listed as one of the background singers.

Obviously, the worries about identification were not particularly strong.

Generally, famous sidemen don't last long in rock. Everybody's ego—and lawyers—won't allow it and a split-up is inevitable. But the Clemons-Springsteen relationship seems to be the exception. They genuinely like each other—"He's my biggest fan," Clemons told me—and they've evolved a working relationship that suits their needs. If Springsteen is the band's conductor, Clemons is its concertmaster, its chief in-house soloist.

If Springsteen is the ultimate rock fan, the one who gets to act out every rock fan's final fantasies, it would seem that he sees in Clemons something of the real thing, the older pro who's lived the on-the-road, kick-around life he writes about.

As for Clemons, he now likes to talk about his marriage and his religious convictions. He grew up in a God-fearing Baptist family in Norfolk, Virginia. With his wilder years behind him, he's settled down. He'll tell you, "I'm in my forties. I'm taking care of myself. But everyone's more serious. The age of the drugged-out rock'n'roller is through. It's not a question of growing old, mind you. I don't feel old, man. The Big Man is ageless."

Ah yes—for those few who already don't know, his present reformed behavior aside, he once developed the reputation as the band's built-in bodyguard, especially during the period in the '70s when Springsteen had left folk behind for rock. At Maryland State College, where he majored in sociology, Clemons also performed as a "killer" defensive lineman, "the most vicious guy on two feet," for the school's football team.

So, some years later, when one surprised promoter or another would demand that Springsteen's E Street Band leave the stage when it was just getting going, Clemons would fix him with a truly evil glare and make a suggestion as to what might happen to the promoter's anatomy should he continue his threats. These threats usually stopped.

Things have settled down considerably, he points out. "There's no one I know who's more dedicated to his art than he [Springsteen] is. He wants everything to be right."

Clemons has his own goals along this line, too. He knows that the mostly rhythm'n'blues-based stuff he plays is not exactly fashionable these days, and he sees his goal in telling rock's younger generation what the first generation was all about.

"Rock'n'roll is a wonderful tool to tell things to our youth," he says. "And there are kids growing up who don't know what emotions, what real emotion, we all used to find in rock'n'roll.'"

Then there's the day that Miami retired. "It's possible that sometime I'll stay on my own for good," Miami was telling me, "but who knows? Who knows?"

One of the main things Miami Steve Van Zandt found out first about Bruce Springsteen was that he "always did precisely what he wanted to do." Well, the same is true of the guitarist himself.

He'd been with Bruce Springsteen when it was called the Bruce Springsteen Band and had had ten pieces—which was early on indeed. But when he began taking his own band out on the road it became increasingly obvious, and increasingly rumored, that he would want to go solo for good.

Little Steven and the Disciples of Soul he called his band. It played clubs a lot and it opened for The Who during the latter's farewell tour. "This is a big band so the size of the place is not a problem," he told me back then. "But opening for The Who was a problem not because we were in arenas but because we were facing their audience, not our own."

Nevertheless, what was crucial was that he create his own identity. It helped

when Springsteen heard his *Voice Of America* album and told him that this was obviously the point for him to go out on his own. (There's an irony here, though. *Voice Of America* is bursting with a kind of red-blooded patriotism that can be found in *Born In The U.S.A.* Van Zandt discovered he felt this way about his country during a sojourn in Europe after he'd recorded his first album, *Men Without Women*. He'd been able to put America, and his feelings about being an American, in perspective. And he'd wanted to put those feelings on record—literally). It also helped make the going easier that he maintained some connection with Springsteen—Van Zandt helped produced *Born In The U.S.A.*

Van Zandt was born in Boston and moved to Middle-town, New Jersey when his mother remarried. He left home and high school about the same time and ended up in Asbury Park. He was passionate about music. More precisely, he was passionate about playing the guitar. The thing that Springsteen remembered about him was that he was constantly practicing. He wouldn't go out for a walk without hauling his guitar along with him, practicing runs, working on his technique as he went.

Steve and Bruce had met some time before they'd started working together.

What they had in common, beyond a passion for rhythm and blues, was their common belief in Springsteen's commitment. They ended up together in the band, Steel Mill, but also worked apart for a while—Springsteen with Dr. Zoom and The Sonic Boom and Van Zandt with The Source. It wasn't until Springsteen's CBS contract and the E Street Band had jelled that they got back together again.

Then there was the return of the bone-fide guitar hero.

Nils Lofgren had been talking about a new recording project, something really interesting. But when given the chance to go out with Springsteen, he had to put everything on hold because the *Born In The U.S.A.* tour was going to last through to the summer of 1985.

He made the decision to join the E Street Band, it was explained, only a month before the tour was to begin. Oh, they'd known—maybe "felt" would be a better word—that Van Zandt had been thinking about splitting for some time. Even so, when it really happened, when the band realized that he really wouldn't be there, it came as something of a surprise. So the courtship of Nils Lofgren began. He'd go over to Springsteen's place and talk. And he'd jam with the band. And he and Bruce would talk some more. Soon enough, though, he was in—and he had to learn something like ninety songs.

He'd been in other bands before and he'd had to learn other repertoires. But this was something else. For one thing, this is one of the tightest units now working—a group that is used to working together. As Weinberg points out, "We all work to Bruce. Sometimes he wants something a bit slower, sometimes he wants it a bit faster. It's always changing and it all comes from him." So Lofgren had to learned something about The Boss's moods as well.

It was bad enough at the start when the kinks were being worked out of the show. But it only got worse three weeks down the road. Lofgren went to dinner with a producer during one of the band's days off—they work three and one-half shows a week on average; that is, three nights one week, four the next—only to return to his hotel room early in the evening.

"But why?" the friend asked.

"I have to study," the guitarist told him. And how. Five additional songs had been added to the repertoire—five more songs Lofgren had to learn, and quickly.

But he also knew what it felt like not knowing all of these songs perfectly. One night, as he was telling a friend down the tour a bit, everything seemed to be going wonderfully. The band was hot. The Boss was hot. Lofgren himself was hot.

So there they were on-stage and Bruce came over and smiled at him, and Lofgran smiled back, and Bruce smiled again and Lofgren, feeling terrific, smiled back again. Then with an even wider smile, Bruce shouted, "It's your solo." Lofgren winced—he'd nearly missed it.

Still, he didn't miss much. If there's ever been such a thing as a rock'n'roll prodigy, Nils Lofgren is it. Born in Chicago (his Italian-Swedish parentage gives him a background not unlike Springsteen's Dutch-Italian origin), he grew up in the Maryland-Washington D.C. area. Even in his early teens he was proving to be something of a kid genius guitar hero. He played with various local bands and eventually formed Grin, with bassist Bob Gordon and drummer Bob Berberich. Grin released its first album in 1971, and its second, *1 Plus 1* the following year. Both were well received critically, if not commercially, yet neither would likely have been recorded had Lofgren not been heard by Neil Young.

Lofgren has often pointed to the Rolling Stones' Keith Richards as one of his influences (look closely to see how great a resemblance there is). And, like Richards, Lofgren is one of the most complete sidemen in rock. It was his work with Crazy Horse and then later on Young's solo album, *After The Goldrush*, which convinced CBS Records there was something there. And there was, but even a third album, *All Out*, failed to attract a big enough audience to find out what indeed was there. Lofgren, again as part of Grin, recorded next for A&M Records and when that didn't catch on either he stayed with the label but went solo, starting in 1975 with the *Nils Lofgren* album, with ace drummer Aynsley Dunbar and bassist Wornell Jones. A half-dozen albums later he was on yet another label—Backstreet Records. And teaming up with Springsteen for the tour to end all tours hadn't stopped him looking for yet another album to do. There he was, a veteran, and still only in his 30s.

bewildering problem of how to keep up. Words tumble over one another, phrases mysteriously feel right and then disappear." The problem, Knobler pointed out, was that everyone had grown used to hearing the formulas used for song writing, the "formulas into which songs and musicians and song writers got routinely thrown." But here was Springsteen doing something that bashed through the formulas— something that ignored them, even when he ended up using them. *Born In The U.S.A.* touches on more song-writing formulas than anything he's done before. But because it's Bruce Springsteen using these formulas, we hear them in different ways. Here they sound deliberate. It's not someone grasping for a way onto the hit parade. The formula points to the song's intention.

Greetings established its own intentions right from the start, too. There was that . . . thickness of sound. This band was just beginning to work together. It was just starting to feel its way. And the band's tightness is only evident on a pair of songs on the album. But already you can hear what it soon was to become. There is Garry Tallent on bass,

The whole theory about Bruce Springsteen is that he came along at just the right time. The theory goes like this—it's the early 1970s, the golden age of rock'n'roll is over, and we're mainly wondering who the next guy in day-glo eyeliner is going to be. In short, we've become rather cynical about the entire process of rock'n'roll. We had become so jaded that when "the backstreet phantom of rock," as Time magazine was to call him in October of 1975, came along, he was immediately given saviorseer status as "the next Dylan." We were looking for heroes and that's exactly what he seemed to be. "If there is a new trend," a Walrus magazine review ran, "look for Springsteen to start it."

But I don't believe that this was, in fact, what happened. Springsteen wasn't the brand-new leader but the consummate follower. (The same still holds true, but to a much lesser degree now; his songs are coming closer and closer to making demands, not just of the singer himself but of his society.) At the start, he was every one of us, male or female, who knew all along that Alice Cooper was just a regular guy but wanted something more than a regular— or irregular—guy.

Well, Springsteen wasn't the next hero, although it wouldn't be too long before that's exactly what he'd become. But in the early '70s, he was something just as important: he established the ground rules for the next hero. And along the way, as critic Paul Williamson once suggested, the singer and his band "are doing for the seventies what Liverpool's Beatles did for the sixties: bringing back rock and roll from the edge of oblivion."

The title of his first album, *Greetings From Asbury Park*, is at once knowingly hip and still slightly tentative. But in a way that was the nature of the man who was behind its songs. Describe Springsteen to anybody—the passion, the lean hips, the croon in the voice, the sensuality that seeps right through the lyrics—and it's difficult not to give a misleading impression, for you end up giving a picture of macho strength and that is not exactly right. Oh, sure, you get the outline down right. The picture catches all the high points and the bright colors, but there's detail being lost in the shadows. This picture misses his gentleness and an old-fashioned sensitivity toward the artistic process. It misses them because he chooses not to reveal them much. (In this he reminds me of those people who hate to have their picture taken and manage every time they're forced into it to somehow cover their face, or turn slightly sideways, or be looking away—as if they don't want something about themselves revealed.) As much as Springsteen believes in the spirit of rock'n'roll and its various attendant shades, he believes in the artistic process. Some of the greatest of all rock'n'roll is played out in the shadows: Elvis Presley slurring his words; Mick Jagger slurring his; Phil Spector's massive studio sound which washed over the lyrics. Ambiguity is a good defense: it allows everyone who wants to to participate—radio stations who want to play the songs and the kids who want to listen —and it keeps out the clods who simply can't figure out what's going on (I mean, just what in blue-blazes is an "interstellar nymph?" I mean, what is this guy saying?)

Ambiguity is something else as well: intriguing. It leads you in and allows you plenty of space to roam around. In *Greetings* Springsteen's lyrics pile meaning on meaning and his voice is cloudy and thick and obscuring. *Good Times* magazine called it "tentative, manic, groping, swirling." He was going after a lot in this album—nothing less than creating a new musical world with its own people, its own scene and its own scenarios. Go-kart Mozart, silicone sister, and early-Pearly. We're in a perpetual Saturday night and it's too late or too early, depending on your needs. Paul Williamson liked saying that, to him, Springsteen and his band signalled "the sixties really are finally over." I think he was right in a way. Ken Emerson in *Rolling Stone* heard the album as sounding "something like Bob Dylan's *Subterranean Homesick Blues* played at 78 rpm." But its street sense is its main link with early Dylan and much in the 1960s. A Springsteen song covers a lot of the same turf a number of earlier rock writers did, but his writing recognizes that a change has occurred on this turf; that there's a rock band playing somewhere. We're never too far from a club in a Bruce Springsteen town, even when we're heading out on the freeway as fast as possible. *Blinded By The Light*, the very song on this very first Bruce Springsteen album which must have jolted everyone who'd picked up the album after looking at its cover—a rather garish greeting card from the almost seedy New Jersey resort town—was a look into chaos. Peter Knobler, writing a review for *Crawdaddy* magazine of a 1973 Springsteen concert at Kenny's Castaways in New York, caught with remarkable accuracy the effect of listening to these early songs saying they "offer that wonderfully creating not just a bottom line but an entire basement of sound that everything else could build on.

Springsteen had been signed by CBS act as an acoustic act—there was nothing wrong about having the next Dylan, especially for the label that still had the first Dylan. Well, Springsteen was was his own guitarist for these sessions and he created that turbulent, layered sound that would remain with him for years; a new kind of rock'n'roll band —one where the guitar did not dominate. (There's probably no direct link from the keyboard dominant E Street Band and that entire generation of synthesizer players which came along later in the 1970s, but certainly the band provided a model for what could be done beyond rock's accepted formula.)

Right from the start, Springsteen thought of it as an early album, a first album. He understood it would be his calling card within the record company which had signed him—CBS—as well as outside it. You can hear its acoustic underpinnings. *Greetings* was sort of what CBS was expecting.

The next album was anything but. To my ears, Springsteen's albums tend to come in pairs. The first of each pair establishes the tone, the second extends the ideas. *Nebraska* and *Born In The U.S.A.* are such a pair: the former's material sounds perfectly in context with the latter's during the 1984-85 tour. *The River* is another pair of albums released as a double-album package. One of these "albums" is a joyous romp through some rock'n' roll; the other is full of songs which pre-figure those which were to appear on *Nebraska*. *Born to Run* and *Darkness On The Edge Of Town* are another such pair. So *Greetings* is paired with *The Wild, The Innocent, And The E Street Shuffle*. The latter is more focused than his debut album — "his writing is not so much verbal paroxysm as definitive image," wrote Lenny Kaye in *Hit Parader* magazine — but the sweep of its vision took in the same sidestreets and the same sidestreet characters the first one did. There's *Little Angel* to head out down the avenue in the company of with that silicone sister from *Greetings*. And it's pretty much the same avenue except for one thing: you can sense Bob Dylan hasn't been down it, at least not recently.

Springsteen had to struggle with all those references to Dylan, especially after the first album came out. If he looked up to any one figure it was Elvis, he would tell reporter after reporter. And if you really wanted to get out of the picture — is now standing there, staring right at us.

Yet nothing prepared everyone for *Born To Run*, the next album. Greg Mitchell, writing in *Crawdaddy*, said that while the songs on *E Street* may not have been as strong as those on the first album, *E Street* nonetheless "emerges as a stronger album, complete unto itself as a presentation of an artist and his milieu." *Born To Run* was an album in this sense and something more — it was the album as rock event. It arrived in 1975, two years after the first pair, and just about the time CBS Records was beginning to think about dropping his contract. The first two had great reviews but few sales. The third album turned it all around. And how. As its songs began to spill out from rock radio stations, there was a mighty media celebration with cover stories in *Time* and *Newsweek* for whom *Time* dubbed "The Backstreet Phantom of Rock."

What was being celebrated on the album itself was a crystallization of many of the singer's ideas. It opens with the story of a young stud who sees what's ahead of him unless he gets out and gets out quick. On *Thunder Road*, the opening song, he begs the girl of his dreams and desire to get in his hot car with him and get out of small studio in Blauvelt, New York, where the first two albums had been recorded. But something was amiss with the sessions and it wasn't until Jon Landau, the critic who had praised Springsteen, had signed on as co-producer with the singer and Mike Appel, was some progress made. Springsteen didn't exactly trust producers but he accepted Landau's suggestion that the album be recorded in the larger and more sophisticated Record Plant studios in New York. Everyone knew that the pattern which had been established with the earlier albums had to be broken. A new method of working was needed.

And this was all the more important because of what Springsteen himself was after — which was nothing less than *Born To Run* to be more than an album — he wanted it to be a *great* album. As it was, it took him over a year to complete, and later he'd come to remember it as the most exhausting time of his life. Songs were worked and re-worked, in the studio with the band and outside the studio. The band itself was still evolving. Miami Steve Van Zandt was still on its fringes, but keyboard player Roy Bittan had arrived to replace David Sancious, and Max Weinberg had settled in as the band's full-time drummer. (A note about

To complicate matters was the growing enmity between Appel and Landau. Springsteen had invited Landau, by now more than a supportive critic by becoming a supportive friend, to sit in on recording sessions. Landau's advice was solicited and accepted. Appel's control was waning, Landau's was rising, but neither fact would matter much unless this album were ever completed. And, for a while there, it seemed as though the album *might not* happen. But Springsteen was going to have his classic rock'n'roll album and nothing, absolutely nothing, was going to stand in his way.

Eventually, nearly everything did stand in his way but the album came out. The struggle and length of time needed to produce it had become so well-known in so many quarters that CBS aimed to build up anticipation for its arrival. The company, using Landau's "future of rock'n'roll" quote, hyped the two earlier albums and they started to sell again. The arrival of *Born To Run* was an event.

But *Darkness At The Edge Of Town* was no less an event. Simply put, it was *Born To Run*'s follow-up album. But there was nothing simple about the way it came about or the way it was received.

But there was almost three years between *Darkness* and the media excitement which had accompanied *Born To Run*. By the time *Darkness* was ready to be started, Jon Landau was fully its producer and Bruce Springsteen was fully aware of what it was like to be a media sideshow. If anything was surprising about *Darkness* was that it came so close in so many ways to the one before it — he'd not given up the drive to make one of the great rock'n'roll albums. Nevertheless, the old idea had been taken a step or two forward here. The people looking for escape — tempting it, trying it — in *Born To Run*, have begun their escape in *Darkness*. Only they don't find the "promised land" they thought they'd find but a dark, often bleak landscape — the landscape which would turn up in *The River* and would be the subject of *Nebraska*. The "badlands" in *Darkness* are forever. They're lived every day. The old hope you might expect with a title such as *Racing In The Streets* has been replaced by a kind of hopelessness — the understanding that the race goes on forever and there's no way out of it.

Prove It All Night has come to be another of the singer's anthem sing-alongs, but the entire album seems too interior to provide much live concert peppiness. (The album also contains one of the best pieces he's written,

down to influences, well, there are Sam Cooke and Wilson Pickett in there too, and Gary "US" Bonds (he still has a car given him by Bonds) and Fats Domino. "I've been influenced by everybody from Benny Goodman on," he told one reporter. On *E Street* they're all a part of his parade past the boys from the casino dance hanging out with the innocent big-city girls along the New Jersey shore. "In fact, not the least of the pleasures of *The Wild, The Innocent And The E Street Shuffle* is that with it he has permanently laid Zimmerman's ghost to rest," wrote Steve Simels in April 1974 in *Stereo Review*, who then went on to invite another comparison to Springsteen: "Clearly we are dealing here with a highly individual *auteur* and, I might add, the first big American rock talent since John Fogerty."

There's something else about the second album, though—it's more deliberately serious than the first. His main forces are all in place: his band and his intentions. For here, starting with *4th of July, Asbury Park (Sandy)* he goes after the epic—nothing less than a hymn to New York City. What was tentative on the first album has become assertive here and the guy who hid in the shadows—the one in the photograph who always seemed to be slightly

town. Despite the sprawling passion in its lyric, the album is neatly balanced, with side two beginning with another version of the *Thunder Road* theme in *Born To Run*. This balance is underlined further with two other songs on the album, *Backstreets* and *Jungleland*. Both look at the world the young stud wants to leave, but while the former is rather more bitter than bitter-sweet the latter song—now one of the main sing-alongs in his repertoire—sensually accepts this world.

An aside here: of all the songs which turn out to be sing-alongs in concert, *Jungleland* is to me, anyhow, the most memorable: a dozen or more times I've heard a crowd sing the lyrics in one vast whisper. It's been haunting at times. Years ago I remember seeing and hearing a British football crowd during a cup match sing an entire Beatles' song while waiting for the action to pick up again. Not many pop artists have been able to make music truly popular in this way—music that can be used, played to, sung-along to, music that's at once intimate and accepted as widely as possible. Starting with *Born To Run*, Springsteen was creating music which more and more worked this way.

But *Born To Run* is a difficult album, in more than one way. It had started as the earlier ones had in a

Weinberg here. Springsteen had had trouble with the exact feel for *Born To Run*. Weinberg, noted *Village Voice* critic M. Mark, "expertly provided the groove Springsteen used to have trouble finding.")

But *Born To Run* is a difficult album, in more than one way. It had started as the earlier ones had in a

Born To Run. There were painful legal struggles for the control of his career—exactly the kind of struggles he'd long tried to avoid, and what was as bad, a deluge of distrustful publicity that followed on the heels of all

Candy's Room, a well-crafted piece that could easily fit on *Born In The U.S.A.*) What attracted as much notice as the album's arrival in 1978 was a piece that wasn't on it—*The Promise*—which Springsteen often performed

Nothing in *The River* was unexpected. With *I'm A Rocker* it gets closer to straight-ahead rock'n'roll than anything he's done in the past, but otherwise in listening to it the familiar patterns and turns and twists and jaunts begin to emerge. This in itself was heartening. If ever there was worry that his gifts might be exhausted or his energy depleted, it can be laid to rest here. If Dylan had come to mean that rock could expand without limits—until he decided to impose those limits himself—Springsteen, by the time of *The River*, had come to mean that its traditions are still fertile. And if anything, *The River* brought Springsteen even closer to rock's traditions.

So there, in *Ramrod*, we catch some vintage Chuck Berry riffs—it's a piece that could have been written twenty years before. *Point Blank* reiterates a much more recent tradition—Springsteen's own. All in all, there is this sense about *The River* that, its length aside, it's a summation for Springsteen: a gathering-in of materials and ideas and in some cases a re-working of them.

But in dealing with Springsteen you deal with process as much as product (a process which never stops. It seems he's either always in the studio working on new material or out on the road

works as one piece (even though some of the pieces could easily fit into *The River* and others do fit nicely alongside *Born In The U.S.A.*).

Nebraska is his coming-of-age. Its cover art is bleak—an empty country road in winter. The music, though spare, is anything but bleak. It's concentrated. A high keening whine of a harmonica begins the first song, *Nebraska*, and that's heard throughout the rest of the album, that and the chording of an acoustic guitar and his voice (yodelling yet) before the song, *Johnny 99*. If the movie "In Cold Blood" were to be made today, this could be its soundtrack.

Now, because of who he was—and what he'd become by the fall of 1982, *Nebraska*'s release date—the ghostly wail of this music whistled down rock radio like a cold wind during a luau. But rock radio, "adult contemporary" or whatever they were calling it, wasn't always happy with *Nebraska*. I mean, here in the dreamy-clouds of radio happy-think were songs about what was happening just outside those radio station doors. So its "bleak and powerful" songs, as one critic described them, were played for a while then overlooked as rumors were spread that the "real" Springsteen album would be out soon, and everyone could then have a good time. Admittedly, *Nebraska*

is also a critic's album: something which attracts wonderful notices which do little to generate sales. But its characters have such life, and their lives are so richly and wonderfully detailed, that the final effect of this work is not for the critic alone but for the fan who has been listening to Springsteen all along.

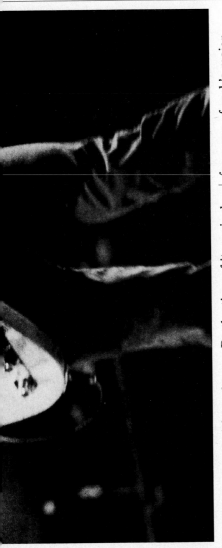

live but he dropped from the album fearing it would be interpreted as a comment on his legal disputes.

The River shows what happened to the hero of *Darkness* after he realized he couldn't storm out of town in his hot car. He's not much older, but he's a lot wiser — and maybe world-weary. *The River* is not an album of action but one of reflection. It deals with what he's thinking about as much as what he's doing. Despite the expansiveness of so many of his pieces — *Cadillac Ranch*, say — this is in so many more ways an interior album. Oh, there's second-guessing and wondering and looking back on other albums. But in *The River* there's also an argument or dialogue which seems to be going on inside the song writer's head. He's arrived at a point where a decision has to be made. He knows what the decision is — he has to move on — the only question is, can he make it?

letting his previous material unfold — there's always evolution.). And as he collected forces for *The River*, as his hero looked at his life and the decisions to be made, a new awareness came from all of this.

Darkness was an album made by a young man. *Nebraska*, released in 1982, was recorded by someone who'd never have those kind of hopes again. *Nebraska*

By the time of its arrival in the fall of 1980, his reputation was at its peak. And *The River* has to be understood in light of that reputation. It was a double album, and for someone as aware of rock's history and the weight given things within this history, he was well aware of how much importance this double album would be given. As well it had a certain immediate value: It was a blueprint for performance. The moment you heard it you could almost see it being worked out live onstage.

By the time of its arrival, Springsteen had emerged as *the* live performer in rock. All those who hadn't liked his music, and still didn't, had to admit that what he did onstage gave another life to the music involved. *The River* needn't be anything other than the ultimate party album and that would have been good enough — at the time. (It may have marked the first time in rock history where what was wanted

from one of rock's major song writers was not just his brand-new songs but a tour which would allow the performance of these songs.) His appearance in the "No Nukes" movie as part of the MUSE concerts held in New York's Madison Square Garden the year before had helped fill the gap, but the live show was what was wanted and as much as any-thing else the arrival of *The River* signalled a tour in the making. Perhaps this helps explain that until the release of *Born In The U.S.A.* his albums have never sold as well as his tours have — as much as his reputation would suggest they should. With *Born In The U.S.A.*, his clout in the marketplace has finally caught up to his reputation — the album was perched on the top of the hit parade charts for weeks. When *The River* came out his career still recalled that of Bob Dylan's in that what he means to rock surpasses what he does in it.

wasn't without hope, certainly. But they weren't a young man's dreams. (Then again, I don't think Springsteen has entirely settled in his own mind his thoughts about growing older. At one time he told me it didn't really concern him, but during the *Born In The U.S.A.* tour he'd count his years — "...31! ...32! ..." but he'd never get to the final number, his current age.)

But there's an irony here. For all its breadth, *The River* is a much smaller album than *Nebraska*. Whatever hopes he'd had for *The River's* acceptance, I doubt it will be considered a key album in his career, as *Nebraska* will likely be (I think, anyhow). Sure, *The River* will show up again and again in concert (*Hungry Heart*, recorded with backing vocals by Flo and Eddy, is another massive sing-along during live shows). It will always be on radio and in people's lives. It's full of fine individual moments. But *Nebraska*

There, in *Highway Patrol-man*, we meet Joe Roberts, who works "for the state." Joe works hard and keeps his nose clean but not Franky. Franky is his brother and is always getting in trouble. So Joe has the devil's own choice — either he has to do the right thing or help his bad brother to escape to Canada to avoid going to trial for a shooting. In *Atlantic City* a guy who gets in too deep in debt ends up working for the mob. In *Johnny 99* a man laid off from work at a Ford plant gets drunk mixing "Tanquery and wine" and kills someone — out of frustration.

Never before have his politics — and here I mean the capital-P variety — ever been so obvious. There's no question that Springsteen is now taking sides and making it clear as to which side he's on. He's an American, right down to his blue collar.

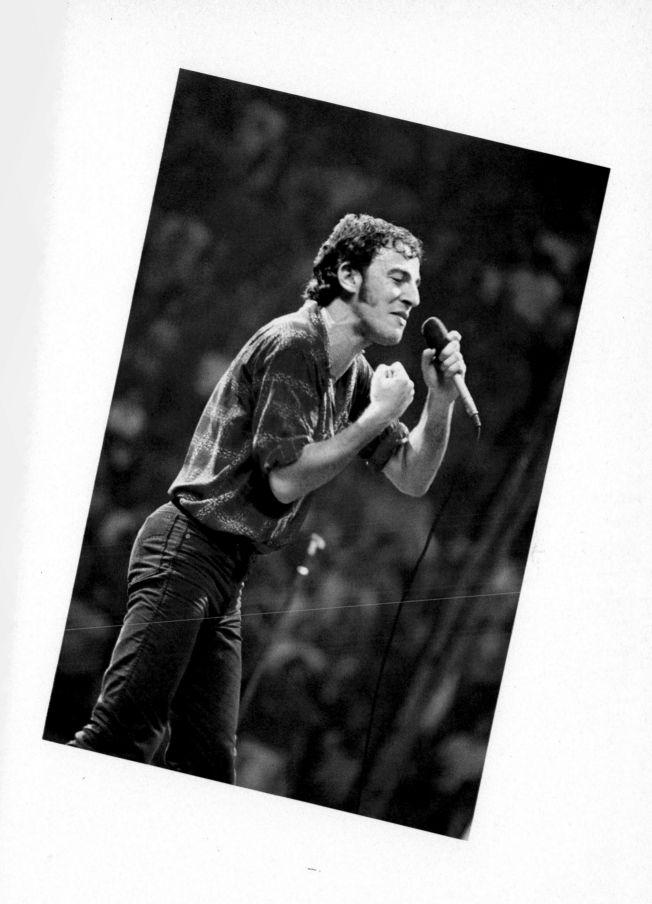

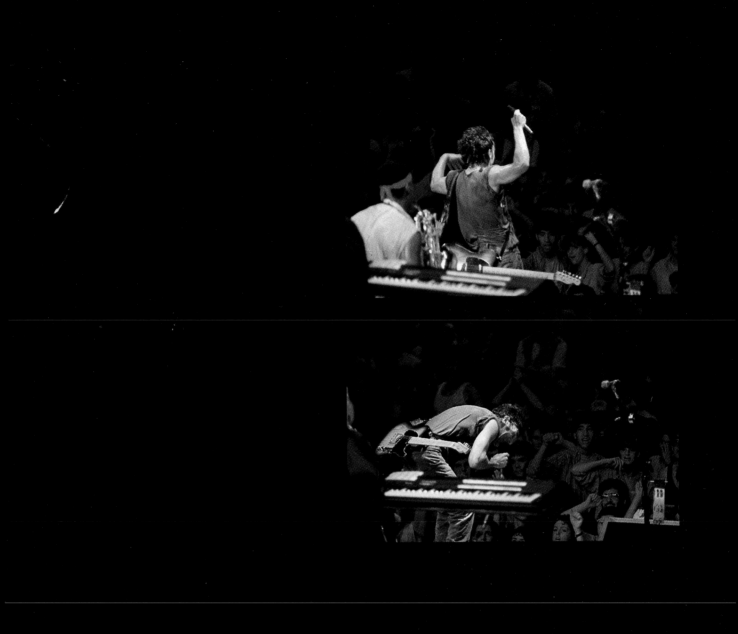

5 THE MAN WHO DROVE OUT OF TOWN

Chicago, November, 1980 There's the sound of some 18,000 whispers here. The audience, it seems, is puzzled.

Bruce Springsteen is about halfway through one of his marathon four-hour concerts, a night that's raged and rocked and gone further than anyone could expect and—what's this?—he's stopped to read a letter. The buzz grows louder.

But what a letter. It begins apologetically, the author realizes that the singer is

midway through a cross-continent tour but would he consider playing a wedding with his band?

Sure, he's big-time now, a $100,000-a-night performer, with trucks, roadies and portable stages and all that. "But the ability to keep up with the wedding circuit is the kind of knowledge no performer should be without," he reads. "We'll pay $50 per player and there'll be an extra $50 for the leader."

You can hear the click of

the ushers' flashlights, it's so quiet in this hall where on most nights De Paul University plays basketball. Might he actually do it?

Suddenly he laughs and we have the answer: No way. A few years ago he might have done that wedding, not for the publicity, but just because it was the kind of thing Bruce Springsteen might do. (Whether he would actually do it or not was irrelevant; what mattered was your belief in him

that he might. Isn't that what he's always been about—belief, his own and his fans'?) But he doesn't do things like that any more. He can't. He's the biggest star in American rock right now—no longer the "last innocent," the dreamer of the sweetest dreams of boardwalk romance on the Jersey Coast, of kids in custom Chevies, born to run.

More than time has passed since he was last out on tour in 1978, playing small halls

in small towns and universities. He has, in his own way, come of age. As he says, "I've discovered there are limits."

It's two hours after the show and he's pacing nervously in a small concrete dressing room. There's a platter of food nearby. He looks pale and tired. "When you're sixteen or seventeen you're never conscious that there are limits to your life, that there is something called age," he says, his hands

Jackson Cage, Fire, Jungle-land, Promised Land and all the songs from *The River* dealing with poor folks doing the best they can. And as he moves, the crowd moves; as he sings, the crowd sings along.

The Who's Peter Townshend has talked about the the rocker's nightmare, of the performer dying onstage and the crowd cheering. Springsteen talks about the dream of being loved by the audience. And in a way he's living this dream. He's communal property.

In a *Village Voice* review of *The River*, Stephen Holden explains its themes in a '50s context. But in a letter to Holden, a Detroit fan named Chuck Wilbur says "like Michael Cimino's 'The Deer Hunter,' [the album] may be an uncomfortable vision for those whose political and cultural sensibilities were shaped by the movements of the '60s."

It's Springsteen asking searching questions of himself. And I realize from now on, in whatever he does, he's going to keep questioning: "I think you come to a point in your life, around when you're thirty, when you look back to the dream you had when you were twenty and you try to assess just where you stand now in relation to that dream."

fanning the air to draw out words when ideas won't come.

"There are signposts. You can drive when you're sixteen and you can drink when you're eighteen—although maybe it's nineteen now in New Jersey—but, whatever, these are just signposts that are telling you the way anywhere. The consideration of age is open-ended. After you're thirty, although you're still pretty young, I think you begin to realize that life is not so open-ended."

That's not the way it was, though. "Each show has such intensity it's as if it's the end of the world," I remember him telling me that wintry night in New Hampshire. His faith has paid off, but with it has come new responsibilities and complications. He's never alone now, not completely. He's always outside there is always the inevitable line-up of deejays, friends, fans from the old days, kids who've never seen him and hard-as-lacquered-nails groupies.

"The last time out we were all pretty green," says Bob Chirmside, his roommate and road manager. "Now we've become a lot more professional."

I've begun to understand something about him. It will

always be like this, in 1984, 1986—whenever. I know tonight I'll be seeing him again in a few years and a few years after that. It's like the river he sings about. It's a constant.

This time he's playing large halls, all sold-out. Radio stations in cities where he's not appearing are taking busloads of fans to concerts in other towns. And Jon Landau has been sent a 15,000-name petition from kids wanting him to go to Winnipeg.

Promoters are now worried about crowd control, not crowd size. His first appearance at Cincinnati's Riverfront Stadium this time around, for instance, was its first sell-out since The Who were there last on December 3, 1982 and eleven fans were trampled to death. He played Milwaukee just nine days after what the police called a "mini-riot" during a Black Sabbath concert. In both cases, though, the concerts went smoothly as he proved that large-scale American rock can work, and peacably.

Tonight in this concrete cavern called the Rosemont Horizon, drearier because it's so new, he's clowning and kidding with the E Street Band, now leaning up against saxophonist Clarence Clemons, now down on his knees for a guitar solo, now up on a ramp waving his fist in the air, singing *Prove It All Night, Independence Day,*

"He's pacing again as I ask, "But isn't rock a young man's..."

"Yes, yes," he says. "It's like baseball. It's like all sports in that when you're thirty-five you're considered an old-timer. But that's just what you're considered. It's not true. This is why I listen to country music a lot because it allows growing up. There's an entire generation in country music that's in its 40s and it's still there, you know."

Lyrics are running through my head, one saying "we're running now," and "I'm a rocker baby," and I wonder, out loud, if all rockers don't have to maintain this tough guy, James Dean, stud-pose?

"Yes, yes," he comes back, "there is that aspect to it but I think that's one of the limitations that's now being knocked down in rock itself. To me, age is no limit. There's [guitarist] Link Wray. I've seen him around little bars in Jersey and he's 51, maybe more. He's as wild as anyone.

"You know what rock'n'roll really is? It's a bunch of people growing older together. It's me and my band going out to the audience tonight and growing older with that audience."

Leaving Paula at her car, I have an hour or so to kill before the show, so I head downtown. I remember something else Woody Guthrie

said: "You ought to watch awful careful to see where the song of your people goes and to go to that direction with your vote." Because every record store I come across has *Born In The U.S.A.* filling the windows—Bruce in red, white and blue. They are his politics, but they are the politics of passion.

Finally, I remember some-

thing Bruce Springsteen had told me, back then in Chicago: "I'm finding that I'm thinking a lot about my parents. You know, for the first twenty years of your life you don't think much about your parents outside of the fact that they're bugging you. You don't think about their lives and you don't think about their particular problems or what

their hopes were or their dreams. How did they succeed? How did they feel? What were their sacrifices? How did it affect you?

"When you were a kid all you wanted was to go out tonight, but when you get older you start to look over everything you really do want. And everything you dreamed."

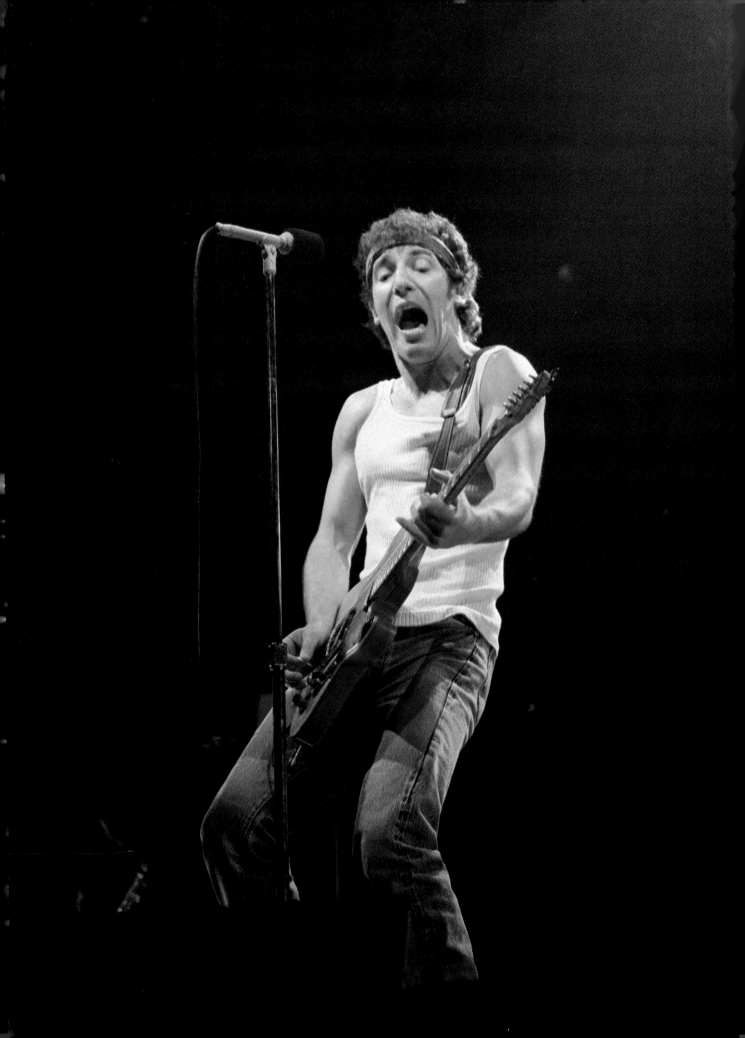

Philip Kamin began photographing rock bands in 1978 when he picked up a camera for the first time and followed Genesis on tour. Since then his photographs have appeared worldwide in magazines, songbooks, programs, publicity campaigns and books, and on album covers and posters. In addition to those groups mentioned in the book list, Philip has also worked with The Cars, The Little River Band, Van Halen, Black Sabbath, Rod Stewart, Teenage Head, Martha And The Muffins, Roxy Music and Ian Dury. A native of Toronto, he makes that city his home.

Philip Kamin uses Canon cameras and equipment exclusively: F1, A1 and T70 bodies with motor drive; lenses: 24mm f/2, 35mm f/2, 50mm f/1.4, 85mm f/1.8, 135mm f/2, 200mm f/2.8, 300mm f/4 Aspherical, 400mm f/4.5 and Canon strobe system.

Peter Goddard is the rock and jazz critic of the *Toronto Star*. He has written for a variety of magazines in Canada, the U.S. and France, and has received a National Newspaper Award for critical writing. Goddard has an M.A. in music and a degree in solo piano performance. He has written several scores for experimental film, including electronic music, and has written and produced for television and radio. Peter, his wife and daughter reside in Toronto, and they spend part of the year on their farm in France. Peter is currently working on a novel, and has been commissioned to write a history of popular music.

Books by Philip Kamin and Peter Goddard
The Rolling Stones Live (In the U.S., *The Rolling Stones: The Last Tour*)
The Who, The Farewell Tour
David Bowie: Out of the Cool
The Police Chronicles
Genesis: Peter Gabriel, Phil Collins and Beyond
Van Halen
Duran Duran Live
Michael Jackson & The Jacksons Live On Tour in '84

By Philip Kamin and James Karnbach
The Rolling Stones in Europe